Spin's Really Really Wild U.S.A. Tour

NATIONAL GEOGRAPHIC SOCIETY

Washington, D.C.

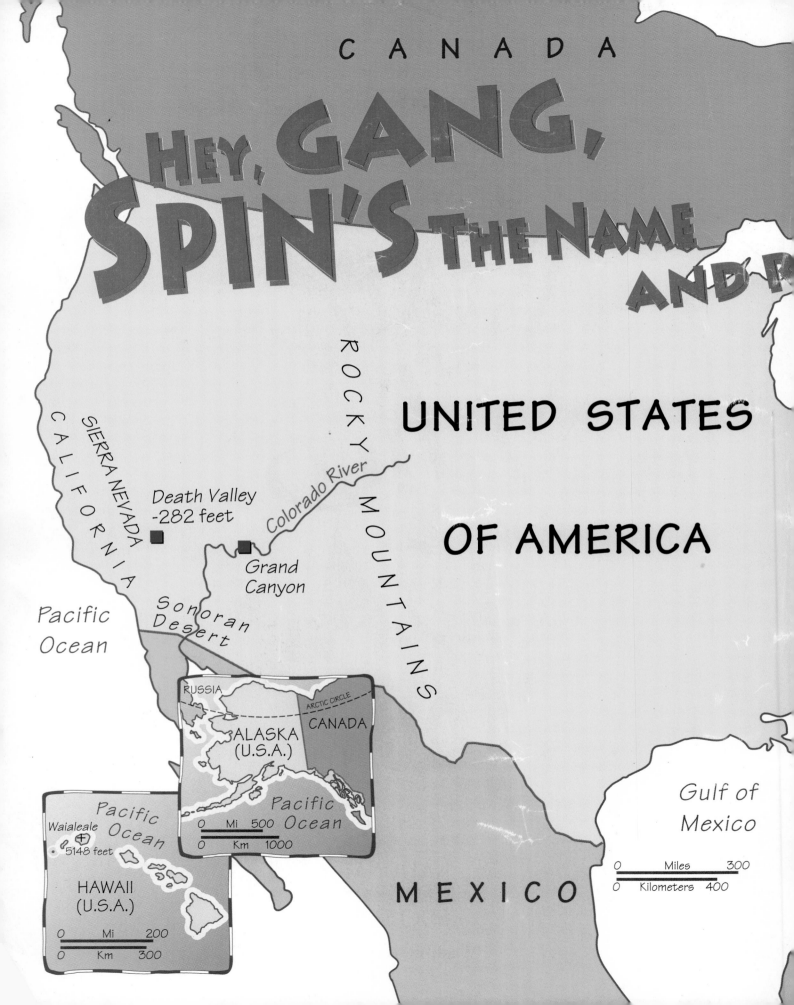

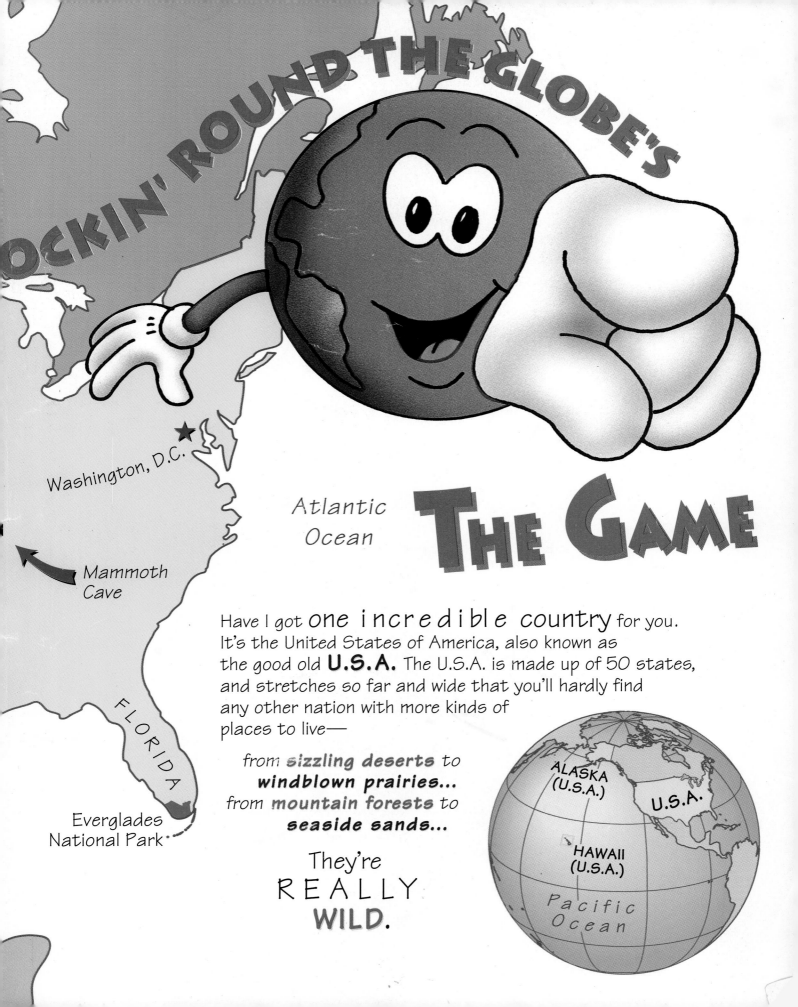

ROCKIN' 'ROUND THE GLOBE'S

THE GAME

Washington, D.C. ★

Atlantic
Ocean

Mammoth
Cave

FLORIDA

Everglades
National Park

Have I got **one incredible country** for you.
It's the United States of America, also known as
the good old **U.S.A.** The U.S.A. is made up of 50 states,
and stretches so far and wide that you'll hardly find
any other nation with more kinds of
places to live—

from **sizzling deserts** to
windblown prairies...
from **mountain forests** to
seaside sands...

They're
REALLY
WILD.

ALASKA
(U.S.A.)

U.S.A.

HAWAII
(U.S.A.)

Pacific
Ocean

If you're ready to tour, I'm ready to be your guide.
So let's spin!

Let's rock this raft down the Colorado River, through the gorgeous Grand Canyon. There are about 100 rapids—mini-waterfalls—on this 277-mile stretch of river.

Whoaa! It's like riding a bucking bronco.

Over millions of years, the Colorado River cut through rock, creating this canyon. Down here at water level, the rock walls are nearly two billion years old. Farther up, where the rocks are only 570 million years old, there are many fossils. **It's like a gigantic graveyard crawling with the fossilized remains of marine life from long ago...** when seas covered this land.

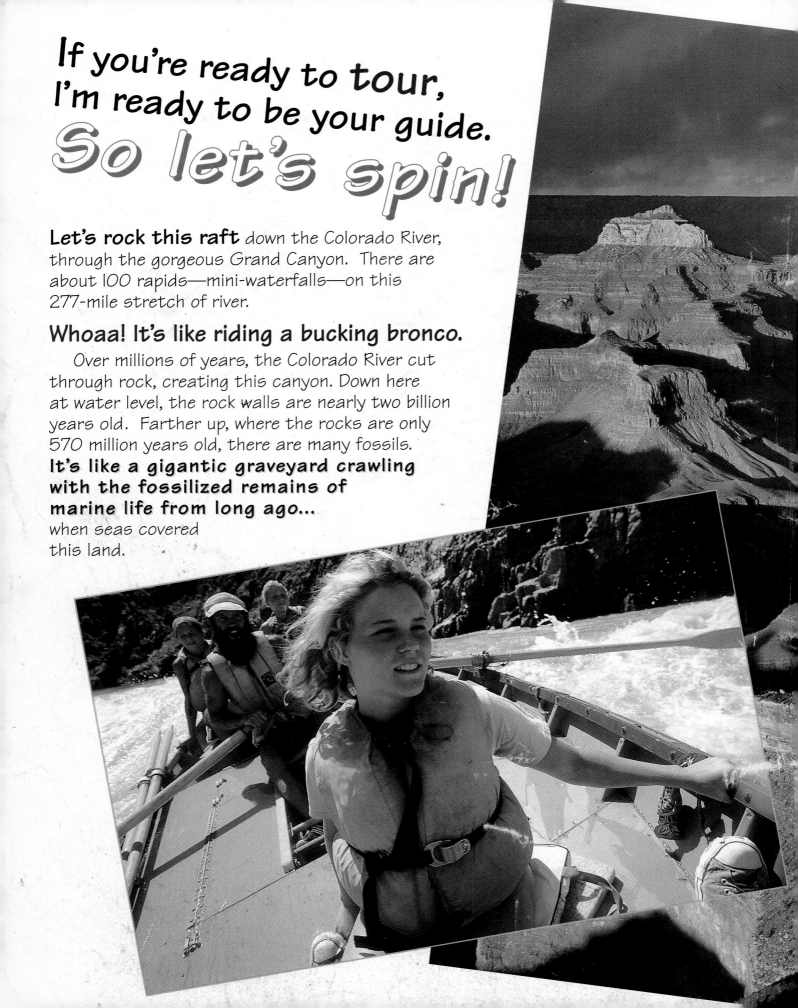

AND UP AND UP...

TO CLIMB HIGH MOUNTAINS

Talk about jagged peaks! Let's fly from the High Sierra (above) to the Rocky Mountains, for a little trek with my mountain goat buddies. On our morning hike, we'll traipse down a sheer cliff, leap over a 100-foot drop, nibble cold delicious mountain grasses...then scramble back up the steep slope to— whoa—check out that mountain lion.

MEET THE KING OF COOL...

The Polar Bear. This dude
lives north—way north—
in Alaska, the northernmost of
the 50 states. This place is really
cool, I mean parts of it can be
minus 60°F cool. Teddy bears
do not make it here.

Lucky for the polar bear
that its big paws are padded. These
big bears can weigh as much as
ten 170-pound humans.

Their thick white fur both keeps
them warm and helps them blend
into their snowy surroundings, so
they can sneak up on seals when
they hunt.

PHEW! THAT'S MORE LIKE IT.

A nice, sunny 116°F hot.

116 hot degrees? Now this is going a little too far. We must be in Death Valley, the driest place in the U.S.A.—with the lowest spot in all the Americas: 282 feet below sea level. Hang around here long enough and you'll end up like this unfortunate skeleton. Before it was a skeleton it was a working **rattlesnake,** one of the meanest hombres out west. You have 26 bones in your spine; some rattlers have 200. Go ahead, count 'em. I'll wait....

SQUAWKING ABOUT THE HEAT?
TRY A CACTUS COOLER

Mmmm. Not bad.

It's 100 percent saguaro nectar—
the specialty drink of the Sonoran
Desert. Like Death Valley, this
is a super dry place. But there's
plenty to wet your whistle,
thanks to the giant saguaro cactus.
Moths drink nectar from the
cactus flowers. So do other
insects, birds, and bats.

A saguaro cactus can live
200 years and **grow to be as
tall as a five-story building.**

For animals, it's like a giant condo.
Woodpeckers carve out holes in the
saguaro, live in them for awhile, then
move on. The elf owl to your right is
nesting in one of these ready-made
rooms. Looks like the squawking
starling on the left has claimed a
home, too.

WESTWARD

This is the place for space. The western U.S.A. covers many thousands of square miles of mountains, forests, deserts, and sagebrush country— or, in Old West lingo, the range. And for *wild mustangs* riding the range is the rage.

This great horned owl is busy **raiding the range.** His flexible neck has 14 bones—twice as many as a human's—so he can turn his head 180 degrees from side to side—and see everything. **SHARPLY.** And not only that...he can swoop down on prey in nothing flat. **KEEP ALERT,** all you desert mice. Little escapes this nocturnal nibbler.

Ho!

If a dive-bombing bird isn't enough to disturb a quiet night, here comes the boom box with a beak: the sage grouse. To serenade its ladylove, the male inflates two sacs on its throat, then deflates them fast. *BOOM!* **You can hear it hundreds of yards away.**

OHH... GIVE ME A HOME WHERE THE BUFFALO ROAM

Hmmm... home getting crowded?
This 12-inch black-tailed prairie dog takes a breather. You would, too, if you shared an underground burrow with dozens of neighbors.

Mmmm... fresh air.
Get ready for aerobics in the wide-open spaces. Then on to find a hearty salad of grasses, a nibble of seeds, and....

Yo, Buffalo! This big bruiser obviously has places to go. Sometimes known as bison, these animals are the heavyweight champs of the North American plains. Large males can weigh in at a scale-crushing 2,000 pounds.

MEANWHILE . . .

In forests across the country, little wild ones are getting a grip. For a **young raccoon,** who was born in a tree hole, heights are happening. A raccoon's front paws have nimble fingers, and its hind paws can firmly grasp a trunk.

Baby bear triplets like a tree, too. It's a great place to find **nuts** or **honey.** Later, little raccoon settles in for a nap. It's quiet time—unless the tree comes crashing down because of the **notorious bark burglar.**

MOST WANTED

THE BEAVER

Alias: Bark Burglar
Also known as: CHOMPERS

Description: Flat-tailed, web-footed, teeth with a tint ➤➤

Profile: One busy body
Previous offense: Clearing trees without a permit

Don't be fooled—those teeth are tough. The orange coating is hard enamel that lets the beaver gnaw through trunks without chipping a tooth. **Definitely don't try this at home, kids.**

In the beaver's defense:

The tree limbs are used to build a dry lodge for year-round living.

CAMERAS READY!

CLICK QUICK!

A mule deer in full velvet won't be in full velvet long. This soft layer of skin protects the deer's newly grown antlers. In just weeks it will peel off, and the antlers will emerge, sharp and powerful. **Then** the deer will lock antlers with other males fighting to win a lovely mate.

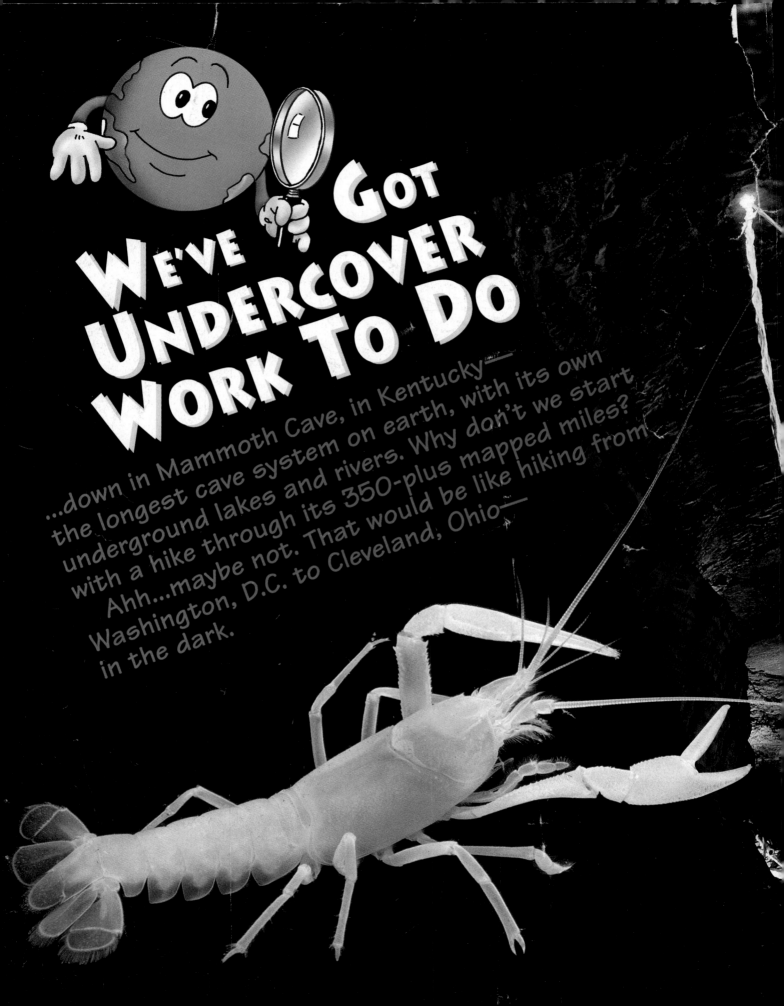

WE'VE GOT UNDERCOVER WORK TO DO

...down in Mammoth Cave, in Kentucky— the longest cave system on earth, with its own underground lakes and rivers. Why don't we start with a hike through its 350-plus mapped miles? Ahh...maybe not. That would be like hiking from Washington, D.C. to Cleveland, Ohio— in the dark.

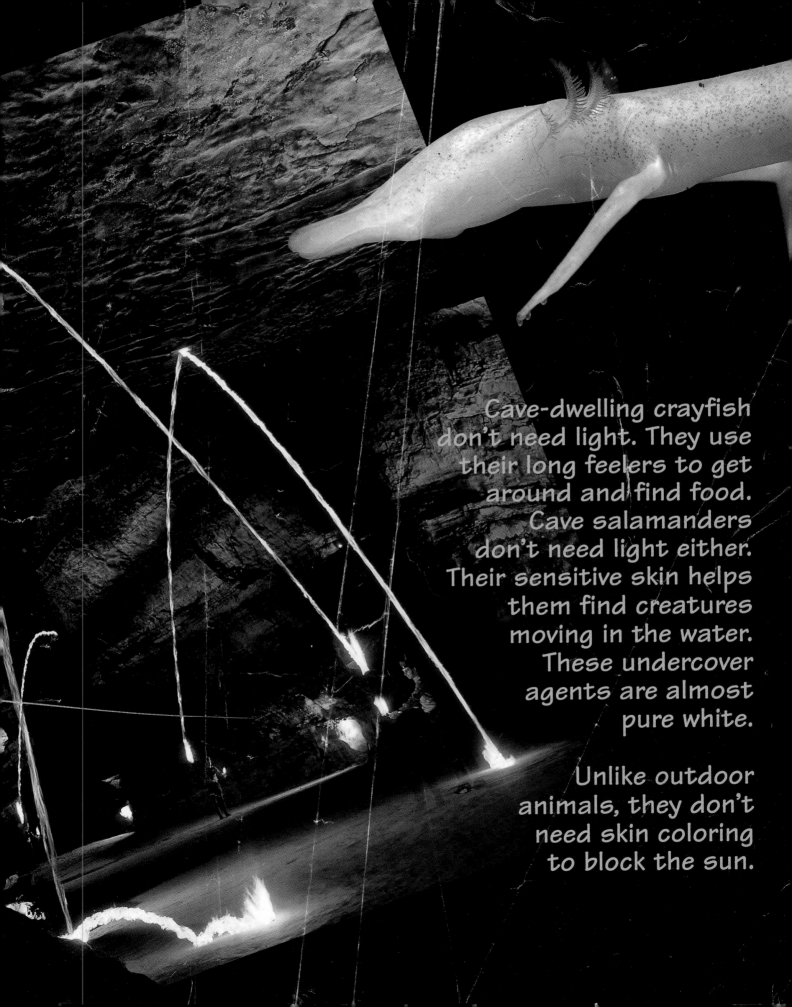

Cave-dwelling crayfish don't need light. They use their long feelers to get around and find food. Cave salamanders don't need light either. Their sensitive skin helps them find creatures moving in the water. These undercover agents are almost pure white.

Unlike outdoor animals, they don't need skin coloring to block the sun.

There's no wilder place than Everglades National Park,

in Florida. The Everglades is the largest subtropical wilderness in the United States, nearly covering the tip of Florida. The Everglades is actually a

wetland

bursting with more weird and wonderful life than you can imagine....

the white heron (top), roseate spoonbill (bottom), poisonous snakes, glass shrimp, fish, frogs, and...

the alligator. Yes, **the gator.**
This fellow can weigh more than <u>four</u> refrigerators
and grow to be as long as a car...
a green, scaly car.
Watch out—a hungry gator is a *fast* gator.

HEY, LATER GATOR!

FAST FOOD BREAK

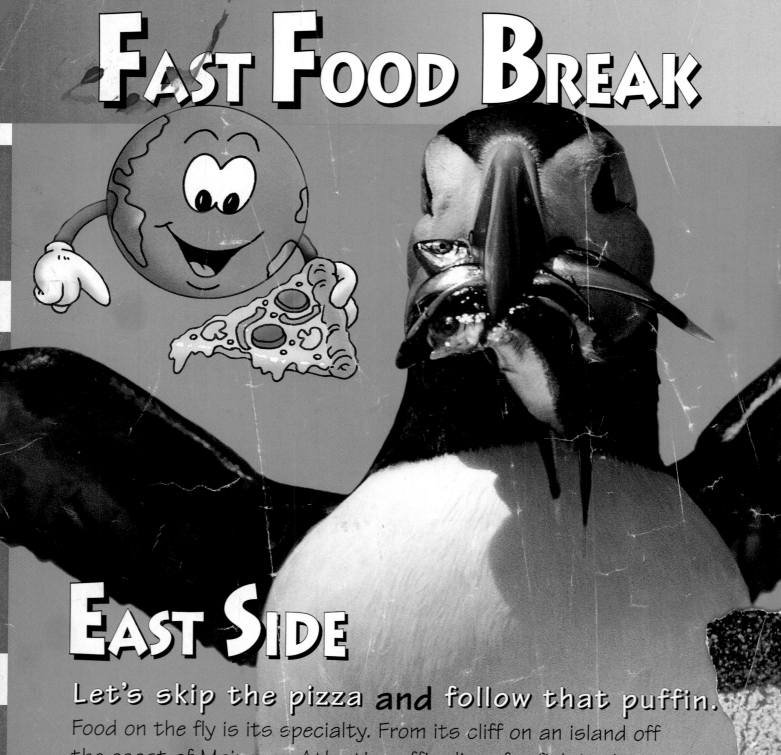

EAST SIDE

Let's skip the pizza **and** follow that puffin.

Food on the fly is its specialty. From its cliff on an island off the coast of Maine, an Atlantic puffin dives for fish in the waters below—and really makes a haul.

Wash down that beakful of fish with a refreshing gulp of ... seawater? Yechh!

Most animals including humans can drink only fresh water. A few birds, including puffins and albatrosses, can drink saltwater, too.

The front cover shows a mountain lion.

Published by the National Geographic Society
Gilbert M. Grosvenor, President and Chairman of the Board
Michela A. English, Senior Vice President

Prepared by the Book Division
William R. Gray, Vice President and Director
Written by Barbara Brownell . Spin Illustrations by Barbara Gibson
Director of Children's Publishing, Barbara Lalicki
Art director, Suez Kehl . Picture editor, Greta Arnold
Map editor, Carl Mehler . Manufacturing manager, Vincent P. Ryan

SPINTM is the host of National Geographic Television's *Really Wild Animals*TM television and home video series for kids. For information on the videos, call 1-800-343-6610, 8 a.m. to 8 p.m. ET, Monday-Friday.
Executive Producer and Vice President, Programming & Production, Andrew Carl Wilk
Director, Children's Television, Cynthia Van Cleef
Associate Producer, Eric R. Meadows

Photo Credits:

Front Cover: D. Robert Franz, THE WILDLIFE COLLECTION; page 4: lower, David Hiser, PHOTOGRAPHERS/ASPEN; pages 4-5: upper, Gordon Anderson; pages 6-7: upper, George Wuerthner; lower, Jim Dutcher; page 7: Ray Richardson, ANIMALS ANIMALS; pages 8-9: Ranulph Fiennes; inset, page 9, John Eastcott and Yva Momatiuk; pages 10-11: ENTHEOS; page 12: Frans Lanting, MINDEN PICTURES; pages 12-13: Farrell Grehan; page 13: lower, D. Lyons; page 14: Jen and Des Bartlett; page 15: Mervin W. Larson, BRUCE COLEMAN INC.; page 16: upper, Jonathan T. Wright, BRUCE COLEMAN INC.; lower, Mitch Kezar; page 17: Jeff Foott; page 18: Rod Planck, DEMBINSKY PHOTO ASSOCIATES; pages 18-19: Jim Brandenburg, MINDEN PICTURES; page 19: Lowell Georgia; page 20: George E. Stewart, DEMBINSKY PHOTO ASSOCIATES; pages 20-21: Carl R. Sams, II; page 21: upper, Stephen J. Krasemann, PETER ARNOLD INC.; lower, Jim Brandenburg, MINDEN PICTURES; pages 22-23: Art Wolfe; page 24: Chip Clark; pages 24-25: David Alan Harvey; page 25: Robert and Linda Mitchell; page 26: upper and lower left, Chris Johns; lower right, James H. Robinson; pages 26-27: Chris Johns; pages 28-29: upper, David Alan Harvey; lower, Frans Lanting, MINDEN PICTURES; pages 30-31: Michio Hoshino, MINDEN PICTURES.

Library of Congress Cataloging-in-Publication Data

Brownell, Barbara
  Spin's really wild U.S.A. tour / [written by Barbara Brownell : Spin illustrations by Barbara Gibson].
    p. cm.
  Summary: A cartoon globe named Spin takes the reader on a tour of the varied regions of the United States,
pointing out the great diversity of plant life, animals, and land formations.
  ISBN: 0-7922-3422-7 (softcover)
    1. Natural history—United States—Miscellanea—Juvenile literature. [1. Natural history—United States—Miscellanea.]
  I. Gibson, Barbara, ill. II. Title.
  QH104.B765 1996
  508.73—dc20   95-44643
                                                                         CIP

NATIONAL GEOGRAPHIC SOCIETY
1145 17th Street N.W.
Washington, D. C. 20036